MOORISH LITERATURE

Moorish Science Temple of America,

PROPHET NOBLE DREW ALI,
FOUNDER

1. THE PROPHET HAS SPOKEN

Friday, November 9, 1928

All Governors and Grand Sheiks and head officials that guide anybody of Moors of any Temple of the Moorish Science Temple of America:

He or she must be of good moral standard and a heart of love and their works must be of Love, Truth, Peace, Freedom and Justice. They are to imitate the Prophet in speech and teaching in any said Temple. They must not be under the influence of intoxicating liquors or any other harmful motive that will terminate to become detrimental to the organization. It must not be known that any leader is staying away from home or neglecting his duty at home or must allow the public to know of their wrong doings. They must forever live the life of Love at home and it must, be known by all the members. They must not speak rash words nor any profane language in the mildest form to any other individual because a leader without influence of good works cannot be a leader, and to be a real Moorish leader you must study the Koran and the Divine Constitution that is handed down unto you by I, the Prophet.

No finance business is to be opened with any group of members of any Temple, by the Governor or Grand Sheik or whosoever in charge without the consultation of I, the Prophet. All uplifting funds, books, are to be issued only through I, the Prophet, because that money is to finance the Moorish Movement.

The head of any Temple can maintain an emergency fund which cannot exceed the amount of from 25 cents to 50 cents a week per member. All public collections and dues also to the supporting of each said Temple and its domestic work.

No finance books are to be served in any Temple except by the Prophet. The head of every Temple must by law obey the word of the Prophet, and if any leader or head of any Temple fails to obey these laws - embezzlement is his charge, and is subject to enforcement of the law by the Grand Body. And the penalty may be a fine or a removal from office, or placed under a very heavy restriction of the law.

Supreme Words of the Prophet, NOBLE DREW ALI.

2. PROPHET DREW ALI SPEAKS TO THE NATIONS

Friday, September 28, 1928

If you have race pride and love your race, join the Moorish Science Temple of America and become a part of this Divine Movement, then you will have power to redeem your race because you will know who you are, and your forefathers were. Because where there is unity there is strength. "Together we stand, divided we fall."

Come, good people, because I, the Prophet, sent to redeem this nation from mental slavery which you have now, need every one of you who think that your condition can be better. This is a field open to strong men and women to uplift the nation and take your place in the affairs of men.

If the Europeans and other nations are helping me, why not you. It is your problem. The Negro problem is being solved only as it can, and that is by the Moorish National Divine Movement. If you have a nation you must have a free national name in order to be recognized by this nation as an American citizen. This is what was meant when it said, "Seek ye first the kingdom of Heaven and all these things would be added unto you."

BY THE PROPHET.

3. A WARNING FROM THE PROPHET FOR ALL GOVERNORS AND GRAND SHEIKS AND HEAD OFFICIALS OF ALL TEMPLES

Friday, October 26, 1928

Renew your acts, amend your ways. Because the great conference is on its way and in it is where the Law will be enforced before the great grand body. The continuance of the present officers in the temple will depend on your past good work. Those who have been delinquent may now know that they will not be tolerated any longer, because this great Divine and National movement must move on according to Law, these things shall be proclaimed.

There is no favorite in any of the temples, for the Law is laid down and everyone who claims a part of the work must be governed accordingly. ALL are one. There is but one Temple in this Nation and there is but one Prophet of the Temples. I come to speak to all Nations, bringing them a message of Love, Truth, Peace, freedom, and Justice. In the Head of every Temple if anyone has violated these Divine Laws it will mean his discontinuance, for no man is to be under the influence of intoxicating liquors nor to seek to tear up the families while under the influence of evil motive; nor must he speak anything that will prejudice the minds of the public against the Divine movement.

If any of the Laws are violated, anybody grand sheik or sheiks can file charge against the violation to the grand body over which the Prophet presides. This power is vested in seven or more sheiks for the protection of your Temple and the Divine movement.

The Prophet Noble Drew Ali

The Founder of the Moorish Science Temple of America

4. THE PROPHET PLEA TO NATION

Friday, March 1, 1929

Our Divine and National Movement stands for the specific grand principles of Love, Truth, Peace, Freedom, and Justice, and I, The Prophet, am applying to all loyal, faithful Moors, members, and the American citizens to help me in my great uplifting acts of uplifting fallen humanity among the Asiatic race and nation, for I have suffered much and severely in the past through misunderstanding of what the movement was dedicated to.

It is the Great God Allah, alone that guides the destiny of this Divine and National Movement. I know all true American citizens are identified by national descent names to answer and apply to the free national constitution of this free National Republic of the United States of America. That's why I am calling on all true national citizens to help me morally and financially in my great work I am doing to help this national government. For without a free national name, without a descent flag of your forefathers, there is not a national divine title of the government in which we live.

This is from your true and Divine Prophet unto all American and foreign sympathizers.

PROPHET NOBLE DREW ALI

5. GENERAL LAWS AS SAID BY THE PROPHET

Friday, November 9, 1928

Every Temple and head is to function by words, deeds, and actions, imitating the Prophet. Especially when teaching a group of Moors, any group of Moors.

These are the General Laws--- the Supreme laws will be handed you to-morrow night. The Supreme Council will be chosen to-morrow, consisting of seven men, tried and true, accepted by you according to their words, works and deeds.

The head of all temples are to give an account once a month of all finances into the Grand Body; and the Grand Sheik---Grand Sheikess---Governor, and Grand Governor of any said Temple are to work hand in hand and intercede that the Prophet is the Law. They are to know they are a part of the law and must obey.

The Heads of all Temples are to by force refrain from all wrath words profanity in the mildest form from his members. They must live the life of Love, Truth, Peace, Freedom, and Justice, and refrain from all alcoholic liquors or any other harmful things that will terminate to destroy Peace, or any other of the Divine Principles. They are not to contribute to anything that will cause the public to disagree with him or her. And for one to lead a group of Moors, you must keep your house clean - - clean with good deeds, kind words-your wives, brothers must hear good words, kind words, and must know of your good deeds. If there are children you must see to their support. Follow this Divine Principle, for if you don't restrict to this Divine Principle then you are not a true Moor, and the heads are not to charge for membership, or to overcharge for cards, buttons, or for anything issued by the Prophet. Those who contribute to either of the preceding are not Moors, but robbers.

Membership, sisters and brothers, is free; not only here but all over the world. The button is 25 cents, card 25 cents; and one month's dues is paid. Every member pays 50 cents a month for dues. This money goes towards the support of the Temple. This, if not paid, does not entitle you to the protection that is provided for you, and especially if you are not working or in the position to work. If you neglect to fulfill this small duty assigned you. How can you rightfully expect money or other help when you are sick or otherwise disable?

And to be a real Moorish leader you must study the Koran and the Divine constitution that is handed down unto you by I, the Prophet.

The head of any Temple can maintain an emergency fund which cannot exceed the amount of from twenty-five cents to fifty cents a week per member. All public collections and dues also go to the support of the Temple and its domestic work. The head of every Temple must, by law, obey the word of the Prophet, and if any head leader or head of any Temple fails to obey these laws -embezzlement is his charge and is subject to enforcement of the law by the Grand Body: and the penalty may be a fine or removal from office, or being placed under a very heavy restriction of the law.

Supreme Words of the Prophet. NOBLE DREW ALI

6. THINK THIS OVER, YOU MOORS

Friday, February 15, 1929

All Sheiks, Grand Sheiks must prepare for the Prophet before he comes to visit them, must see to it that all is clean and in perfection as far as comfort is possible or otherwise don't arrange to have his presence. All members should pay from 25 cents to 50 cents weekly towards the Emergency Fund. This fund will increase so that it will soon amount to the grand sum of $1,000. That is, if you are loyal Moors. The Emergency Fund goes into the bank. The treasurer will tend to the responsibility of seeing that the money is in the bank, yes, and under the name of the Moorish Science Temple of America Finance. When needed, act according to the law pertaining to the procedure of performing an Emergency Act.

No head of any said Temple is to borrow from any member more than five to ten dollars unless by notification of the Prophet, the necessity for the loan. When any said Temple desires to purchase property they must first notify the Grand Body or the Prophet and it must be purchased under the name of the Moorish Science Temple of America or Noble Drew Ali. An individual name should never be applied. I, Noble Drew Ali, am responsible for all finance, so therefore let I, the Prophet, know what is on me.

Some of you have slipped and slipped drastically, so you had better lace up your shoes before I get there. Everything, every business transaction or anything pertaining to finance is to be transacted in the name of the Moorish Science Temple of America, or Noble Drew Ali. We Moors must maintain a grand treasurer, just as in the days of our forefathers; then you are a nation-until then, you are nothing.

The Emergency Fund is issued by no book, but by an emergency card punched according to contribution, then marked on book; that is the law, and the law must live. The government is behind me, and I must get behind you. For I must uphold and enforce the law, my mission is to save you Moors.

The heads of all Temples, Grand Sheiks, and Grand Sheikess must confirm to the Divine principles: Love, Truth, Peace, Freedom, and Justice. They must live the life among the members and be loved even as the Prophet is loved. They must not practice the principle of segregation among any group in his or her Temple. Let it be he or she that is head of any Temple of the Moorish Science Temple of America that if there should come any grievance that cannot be settled by the head, notify the Prophet at once.

No member is to attend Adept Chamber that has not lived a moral and clean life, and has not paid his or her dues or assessments, providing that he or she is working or able, cannot consider himself a Moor. But traitors must be excluded from the books after having fair trial by the head of their Temple, and that must be sent into the Grand Body. And all members that are able to, subscribe towards the uplifting fund because it takes finance to uplift a nation. And those that are able and fail to act, are not Moors, but traitors to their cause and trust and their nation, and are not allowed to share all the Moorish honors. And the penalty is-- It is embezzlement of the faith of our creed. All heads of all Temples must observe these laws.

BY THE PROPHET.

7. TEMPLE TAX NECESSARY CONVENTION VOTES-UNAMIMOUSLY-TAX PAID MONTHLY

Friday, October 26, 1928

Because of the fact that the expense of the operation of the Temple is increasing so fast, that it was found necessary to vote a tax to the Prophet to carry on the work. This idea was concurred with by the Supreme Grand Council. This act is so arranged that it will not be a burden to any of the Temples, but the Prophet is very emphatic that it shall not be ignored.

The expense of operation has heretofore been taken care with funds received from the manufacturing department, and it was found that it was a burden on that department. Hence, the tax was necessary. This tax is twenty-five cents ($.25) per month per capita. This will mean that the numerical strength of the temple will bear the proper share of the responsibility of operation.

This per capita tax is intended to supply all members alike. Governors and Grand Sheiks included.

The Governor or officer in charge of each Temple will cause a report to be rendered to the Supreme Grand Business Manager of the Supreme Grand Council, 3140 Indiana Ave., Chicago, which will specify and itemize the following: number of Adepts, number of members, number of new members taken in each month or those who join after the rendition of the last report. Twenty-five cents must accompany the name of each. Such members as the representation tax.

The per capita tax collection begins November 1, 1928. All concerned will save themselves penalized if they render their reports promptly and specifically, because otherwise it will necessitate a representative calling on such delinquent Temples an auditing their books, which expense will be borne by the Temple. All Governors and other officers will be held responsible for the representation tax and report.

By order of the Prophet Noble Drew Ali

8. PROPHET WARNS ALL MOSLEMS-GOVERNORS ORDERED TO READ PROCLAMATION AT EACH MEETING

Friday January 15, 1929

I, hereby inform all members that they must end all radical agitating speeches while at work in their homes or on the streets. We are for peace and not destruction. Stop flashing your cards at Europeans; it causes confusion. Remember your card is for your salvation. Failure to obey these orders will be of severe consequence.

We are for Love, Truth, Peace, Freedom, and when these principles are violated, justice must then take its course.

Any member or group of members who hold malicious feelings toward the temple or the Prophet, or violate the divine covenant of the Moorish Movement will receive their reward from Allah for their unjust deeds.

All true Moors will and must obey the law as laid down to them by their Prophet. If they lose confidence in their Prophet, they should turn in their card and button, cease wearing their turban and fez and return to the state where I, the Prophet, found you.

This is a holy and divine movement founded by the Prophet Noble Drew Ali, and if the Prophet is not right, the temple is not right.

The Prophet, therefore, is sending out the divine plea to all Moorish Americans that they do their part in protecting their Prophet and the Temple.

This is an everlasting movement founded by the Prophet through the will of "Allah" to redeem his people from their sinful ways.

"NOBLE DREW ALI."

9. WHAT SHALL WE CALL HIM?

So often our various journalists find trouble in selecting the proper name for the Moorish American. Some say "Negro," another will brand him "Race Man," still another will call him "Afro-American," and then come "Colored," "Dark American," "Coon," "Shine," "The Brethren," and your "Folks." It is indeed a hard matter to find something suitable for the various occasions where a title needs to be used. Is it that these people have no proper name? Did they have a National name when first brought to these shores in the early part of the Seventeenth Century? If so, what was it? Did not the land from which they were forced have a name? It now appears a good idea for those whose duty it is to write for the various journals to find out what the National Name of the forefathers of these people was.

Also look into the history of the founders of civilization and see who they were and where they stood in the building of the present civilization. Probably two hours in an up-to-date library would serve to relieve the strain on our men of letters. When the occasion presents itself for a title for these people. The matter of the various names given to these twenty-two million people with all colors of every race of the globe was an act of European psychology. They gave him a name, then defined it as something inferior to theirs, "White," they defined as a color of purity; "Black," they say represents everything of evil. The

"Negro," as they were called in this nation, have no nation to which they might look with pride. Their history starts with the close of the Civil war or more properly with his being forced to serve someone else. Thus he is separated from the illustrious history of his forefathers who were the founders of the first civilization of the Old World. This matter should be looked into with a hope of correcting it.

10. A DIVINE WARNING BY THE PROPHET FOR THE NATIONS

The citizens of all free national governments according to their national constitution are all of one family bearing one free national name. Those who fail to recognize the free national name of their constitutional government are classed as undesirables, and are subject to all inferior names and abuses and mistreatments that the citizens care to bestow upon them. And it is a sin for any group of people to violate the national constitutional laws of a free national government and cling to the names and the principles that delude to slavery.

I, the Prophet, was prepared by the Great God Allah to warn my people to repent from their sinful ways and go back to that state of mind to their forefathers Divine and National principles that they will be law-abiders and receive their divine right as citizens, according to the free national constitution that was prepared for all free national beings. They are to claim their own free national name and religion. There is but one issue for them to be recognized by this government and of the earth and it comes only through the connection of the Moorish Divine National Movement, which is incorporated in this government and recognized by all other nations of the world. And through it they and their children can receive their Divine rights, unmolested by other citizens that they can cast a free national ballot at the polls under the free national constitution of the States Government and not under a granted privilege as has been the existing condition for many generations.

You who doubt whether I, the Prophet, and my principles are right for the redemption of my people, go to those that know law, in the City Hall and among the officials in your government and ask them under an intelligent tone, and they will be glad to render you a favorable reply, for they are glad to see me bring you out of darkness into light. Money doesn't make the man; it is free national standards and power that makes a man and a nation. The wealth of all national governments, gold and silver and commerce belong to the citizens alone and without your national citizenship by name and principles, you have no true wealth, and I am hereby calling on all true citizens that stand for a National Free Government, and the enforcement of the constitution to help me in my great missionary work because I need all support from all true American citizens of the United States of America. Help me to save my people who have fallen from the constitutional laws of the government. I am depending on your support to get them back to the constitutional fold again that they will learn to love instead of hate, and will live according to Love, Truth, Peace, Freedom, and Justice, supporting our free national constitution of the United States of America.

I love my people and I desire their unity and mine back to their own free National and Divine standard because day by day they have been violating the national and constitutional laws of their government by claiming names and principles that are unconstitutional. If Italians, Greeks, English, Chinese, Japanese, Turks, and Arabians are forced to proclaim their free national name and religion before the constitutional government of the United States of America, it is no more than right that the law should be enforced upon all other American citizens alike. In all other governments when a man is born and raised there and asked for his national descent name and if he fails to give it. He is misused, imprisoned, or exiled. Any group of people that fail to answer up to the constitutional standards of law by name and principles, because to be a citizen of any government you must claim your national descent name, because they place their trust upon issue and names formed by their forefathers.

The word Negro deludes in the Latin language to the word nigger; the same as the word "colored"' deludes to anything that is painted, varnished and dyed. And every nation must bear a national descent name of their forefathers, because honoring thy fathers and thy mothers, your days will be lengthened upon this earth. These names have never been recognized by any true American citizens of this day. Through your free national name you are known and recognized by all nations of the earth that are recognized by said national government in which they live. The 14th and 15th Amendments brought the North and South in unit, placing the Southerners who were at that time without power, with the constitutional body of power. The free national constitutional law that was enforced since 1774 declared all men equal and free, and if all men are declared by the free national constitution to be free and equal since that constitution has never been changed, there is no need for the application of the 14th and 15th Amendments for the salvation of our people and citizens.

So, there isn't just one supreme issue for my people to use to redeem that which was lost, and that is through the above statements. Then the lion and the lamb can lie down together in yonder hills. And neither will be harmed. Because Love, Truth, Peace, Freedom and Justice will be reigning in this land. In those days the United States will be one of the greatest civilized and prosperous governments of the world. but if the above principles are not carried out by the citizens and my people in this government, the worst is yet to come, because the Great God of the Universe is not pleased with the works that are being performed in North America by my people and this great sin must be removed from the land to save it from enormous earthquakes, diseases, etc.

And I, the Prophet, do herein believe that this administration of the government being more wisely prepared by more genius citizens that believe in their free national constitution and laws and through the help of such classes of citizens. I, the Prophet, truly believe that my people will find the true and Divine way of their forefathers, and learn to stop serving carnal customs and merely ideas of man, that have never done them any good, ,hut have always harmed them.

So, I, the Prophet, am hereby calling aloud with a Divine plea to all true American citizens to help me to remove this great sin which has been committed and is being practiced by my people in the United States of America, because they know it is not the true and Divine way and without understanding they have fallen from the true light into utter darkness of sin, and there is not a nation on earth today that will recognize them socially, religiously, politically or economically, etc. in their present condition of their endeavorment in which they themselves try to force upon a civilized world, they will not refrain from their sinful ways of action and their deeds have brought Jim-Crowism, segregation, and everything that brings harm to human beings on earth. And they fought the Southerner for all these great misuses, but I have travelled in the South and have examined conditions there, and it is the works of my people continuously practicing the things which bring dishonor, disgrace, and disrespect to any nation that lives the life. And I am hereby calling on all true American citizens for moral support and finance to help me in my great missionary work to bring my people out of darkness into marvelous light.

-FROM THE PROPHET.

11. RELIGIOUS CONTROVERSY

In this age there is still much religious controversy as to the right thing.

Big and powerful ministers have come to the conclusion that something is wrong. Some say it is the Ten Commandments, others say there is a lack of sincerity in the purpose of the churches; still others think it is all worthless and not fit for the time it takes to attend them. However or whatever their final decision might be, it is certain they will make a change or rather try to make one.

The fact of the matter is that they have always had only a reflection of the truth and not the real thing. Like one who holds up to the sun a mirror and casts a few of its diverted rays in a different direction, so have they done with the truth that is supposed to have come from the East.

There are but few people who know what the truth is about man, and that few know that it is foolish to try to impart it to the ignorant. Although the ignorant has finished college, he is a fool right on, being trained to jump through a hoop. The longer he stays in the schools, the better he can jump, and the more he defends his jumping.

From the East comes all light, but though the sun is hanging at high noon; the blind cannot see. The same as the Islamic Creed from the East was brought to the Asiatics of America by the Prophet, NOBLE DREW ALI, and offered to those who were sick at heart, tried for many years, yet they are blind and cannot see the light, Nor is the Prophet trying to put new wine in old skins, for he knows that it will burst them. Still he has the only remedy for the nations. The remedy brought by Jesus, Mohammed, Confucius, and all of the other prophets, which remedy is truth.

The nations do not want the truth; it is too stern, but until they accept it and find out where it is, there will continue to be religious controversy.

12. SAVIOUR OF HUMANITY

In this electrified age men are racing into this life without complete knowledge of where they are going, or what the end will be, when riches seem to be their only pursuit, to be obtained anyway and at any cost; when selfishness, avarice, greed and lust dominate their very being; when humanity in general is left at the mercy of those who have no mercy in them. It is truly wonderful and astounding to see one come into this mad human drama for the sole purpose of saving humanity. Losing all sight on those things worldly and yielding absolutely to a cause higher than has ever yet been attained. This picture is the likeness of Prophet Noble Drew ALI, who is serving humanity.

Coming as he does with a message for the nations in somewhat the same manner as did Jesus, Mohammed, Buddha, Confucius and other prophets of their day. Only the things of this prophet's day differ from the ills of the days of the past; and yet the remedy for the ills of today is about the same as the remedies for the days past; all turning about the pivot Love -love for humanity.

Humanity must be lifted from the unwholesome depths of poverty, misery and suffering and placed on the solid rock of salvation. There are some who claim to do this but upon investigation, one finds that they have slouched under the wings of their cross to extract from those who come to them, means by which they can have the pleasures of this life, while they point their followers to joy after death. While they "feed their sheep" they also shear them while eating. At the close of their day the Master will be heard to tell them, "You have your reward, get thee hence."

Rare is it that you find a real prophet whose mission is the salvation of the nations. The land is full of false prophets whose mission is to fleece the people.

The time was and now is that there should come into the land a prophet in the likeness of his brothers, to redeem them from sin and slavery. Truly this Prophet Noble Drew Ali is the man, bringing with him the message of Love, Truth, Peace, Freedom, and Justice. This alone can save the nations. Like the coming of Jesus, he does not come from the elect, nor the rich, nor the mighty in worldly power, but all power is given unto him to do good. This power is from Allah.

It will be his works that will make men of every nation accept the truth that he brings. It will be through his teachings that the nations of the earth will understand the will of the Master; it will be through him that "Peace on earth and good will to all men" shall come. It will be through his work that humanity will be brought from the slime of life and placed on the solid rock of salvation.

13. WHAT IS ISLAM?

Friday, February 1, 1929

Islam is a very simple faith. It requires man to recognize his duties toward God Allah, his Creator and his fellow creatures. It teaches the supreme duty of living at peace with one's surroundings. It is preeminently the religion of peace. The very name Islam means peace. The goal of a man's life, according to Islam, is peace with everything. Peace with Allah and peace with man.

The Koran, the Holy book of Islam, tells us that the final abode of man is the "House of Peace." 'where' no vain word or sinful discourse will be heard. The Holy Divine Prophet, Noble Drew Ali, says that a follower of Islam in the true sense of the word is one whose hands, tongue and thoughts do not hurt others.

Object of man's life, according to Islam, is its complete unfoldment. Islam teaches that man is born with unlimited capacities for progress. Islam does not support the idea that man was born in sin. It teaches that everyone has within him the seed of perfect development and it rests solely with himself to make or mar his fortune.

The cardinal doctrine of Islam is the unity of the Father-ALLAH. We believe in one God. Allah who is All God. All Mercy and All Power. He is perfect and holy, All Wisdom, All Knowledge, and All Truth. These are some of His great attributes so far as we can understand.

He is free from all defects, holy and transcendent. He is personal to us in so far as we see His attributes working for us and in us; but He is nevertheless, impersonal. Because He is infinite, perfect, and Holy, we do not believe that death, decay, or sleep overtake Him. Neither do, we believe that He is a helplessly inactive and inert force. Nothing happens without his knowledge and will. He neither begets nor is He begotten, because these are the trails of frail and weak humanity.

This unity of Allah is the first and foremost pillar of Islam and every other belief hangs upon it.

14. CAVEAT EMPTOR

Friday, March1, 1929

Moors are men, upright, independent and fearless who care for their loved ones and follow the Prophet to a destiny which is neither uncertain nor unknown. They are fortified by the impregnable doctrine built upon Love, Truth, Peace, Freedom and Justice. It is therefore, folly at its greatest height for smelly culprits with their insidious plans to invade such realm.

They try and try but their own bad planning brings down wrath upon their heads like the sword old Damocles had. Intrigue and scurrilous cunnings find a difficult path to travel within the ranks of the Moors. This is so because the Moorish Movement has been well planned by Prophet Noble Drew Ali, whose latent powers are abundant, unknown and may be called into action, as a matter of defense, at any moment.

Prophet Noble Drew Ali knows the people within his ranks who are interested. They are the vanguard of the Movement as the Moorish hordes increase here in America. All of the Moors are active not passive. A member's interest can only be in one direction and having traveled over the road years before the Prophet knows where every member is along the road.

A few feet below is another road where schemers work, where traitors grin, and culprits bask in the sun. They think they are on the same road with true Moors, but the Moors are high above on a pinnacle where they might view the destructionists as they fall for the last time and their bones bleach in the sultry mid-day sun.

Hungry scavengers flying high, catch scent, devour and leave crying out: Caveat Emptor - - cast out the dead carcass. The Moors high above see these plotters, purveyors, the worst that exist, hurl themselves downward by their own works as the hawks wait.

15. PROPHET ANNOUNCES HIS AUTHORITY AND POWER

Forced to make changes. All Governors and other officers of the Moorish Science Temple are hereby congratulated for their past loyalty and fidelity, for I know it will be the same in the future. Because of certain incidents that have arisen in some of the Temples which seem to come from the fact that there are those who do not know where the seat of power is vested the Prophet has ordered the following to be published;

All authority and power of the Moorish Science Temple of America is vested in the Prophet Noble Drew Ali and those whom he appoints to act as in the Supreme Body. The Prophet has the authority and power to expel any officer or member of the Moorish Science Temple of America who willfully violates or refuses to comply with the rules in regard to branch Moorish Science Temple. And such suspensions and expulsions shall stand until in the judgment of the Prophet, the members and officers shall have made satisfactory atonement. All officers and members of the Moorish Science Temple of America and such rules and regulations of the constitution shall be in writing and not at variance with any law of the city, town or nation which the prophet shall declare a law.

During this session of the convention, all rules, regulations, and laws of the constitution and such as might be enacted and ordered by the Prophet, shall express and explain in detail, so there can be no doubt as to what is required of each and every officer or member of the organization.

The Prophet will positively not tolerate any interference with the operation of this National Divine Movement from anyone.

By the Prophet, NOBLE DREW ALI.

16. PROPHET SENDS MARRIAGE LAW TO ALL TEMPLES

Friday, March 1, 1929

All marriage ceremonies of members of the Moorish Science Temple of America must be performed by an ordained minister and the head of the temple.

And any man desiring to take unto himself a wife and receive our Moorish rites, he must go to the City Hall and receive his license to be registered in that city, county, and state. It then must be turned over in the hands of the aforesaid ordained minister and head of a temple after it has been properly signed by city officials. The price thereby for such administering to man and wife will be five dollars. For all those who have their papers and desire our Moorish marriage ceremony, it is three dollars.

We Moors cannot marry anyone but we obligate you according to our divine laws and covenant and the laws of the land. This must be proclaimed and made known to every temple so that there will be no misunderstanding. There will be no misunderstanding about I, the Prophet, and my teachings because Allah alone binds two hearts together as a unit. These are the marriage obligations and instructions for man and wife.

Chapter 22 from our Koran is to be read first to the husband and chapter 21 is to be read secondly to the wife. These are the instructions of marriage from our Holy Koran. Please obey the law as given you by your Prophet through your Governor.

PROPHET NOBLE DREW ALI

17. MOORISH COSTUMES BALL

Friday, October 26, 1928

So enthusiastic was the reception of the costumes worn by the Moorish Americans during their parade that the members of the Moorish Science Temple have decided to have at different times what they will call a Moroccan Costume Ball. This affair will be had shortly after the holidays, about New Year's Eve. The Prophet consented that this could be for the entertainment of the members. Other groups of people in the city have been using the dress of our forefathers and imitating them all but the olive hue they cannot get.

During the Moorish convention more than fifteen hundred Moroccan costumes were rented to Europeans who had seen the program and knew the Moors were to have a costume parade. But, nevertheless, we were successful in obtaining through certain Asiatic costume dealers, all the costumes we wanted.

The Moorish Costume Ball will be among the first of such given where an idea is put forth that has to do with the origin of the millions of people in this country, who can trace their ancestors back to the illustrious founders of civilization. It will remind the descendants of these people of the time when their forefathers were the main people to spread the most progressive ideas of civilization. In fact they paved civilization many times.

When more barbaric tribes from the North were ravishing all countries, they were permitted to enter. It was the forefathers of the Moorish Americans and their near kin that saved the historic records that were threatened during the days when the burning of libraries was a fad for despotic soldiers.

This costume ball will be much looked for and appreciated.

BY THE PROPHET.

18. THE INDUSTRIUS ACTS OF THE MOSLEMS

The Industrious Acts of the Moslems of Northwest and Southwest Africa

These are the Moabites, Hamathites, and Canaanites who were driven out of the land of Canaan by Joshua, and received permission of the Pharaohs of Egypt to settle in that portion of Egypt. In later years they formed themselves kingdoms. These kingdoms are called this day Morocco, Algiers, Tunis, Tripoli, etc. They originated the beauties of the Alhamhra and to an unpracticed eye the light relives and fanciful arabesques which cover the walls of the Alhambra appear to have been sculptured by the hand. With a minute and patient labor, and inexhaustible variety of detail, yet a general uniformity and harmony of design truly astonishing. And this may especially be said of the vaults, and cupolas which are wrought like honeycombs or frost work, with stalactites, and pendants which confound the beholder with the seeming intricacy of their patterns. The astonishment ceases, however, when it is discovered that this is all stucco work, plates of plaster of paris cast in moulds and skillfully joined so as to form patterns of every size and form. This mode of disappearing walls with arabesques and stuccoing the vaults with grotto work was invented in Damascus but highly improved by the Moors in Morocco to whom Saracenic architecture owes its most graceful and fanciful details. The process by which all this fairy tracery was produced was ingeniously simple. The walls in their naked state were divided off by lines crossing at right angles, such as artists use in copying a picture. Over these were drawn a succession of interesting regiments of circles. By the aid of these the artists could work with celerity and certainty and from the mere intersection of their plain and curved lines arose the interminable variety of patterns, and the general uniformity of their character. Much gilding was used in the stucco work, especially of the cupolas, and the interstices were delicately penciled with brilliant colors, such as vermilion and lapis lazuli laid on with the whites of eggs.

The primitive colors alone were used, says Ford, by the Egyptians, Greeks, and Arabs, in the early period of art, and they prevail in the Alhambra wherever the artist has been Arabic or Moorish. It is remarkable how much of their original brilliancy remains after the lapse of several centuries. The lower part of the walls in the saloons to the height of several feet is encrusted with glazed tiles, joined like the plates of stucco work so as to form various patterns. On some of these are emblazoned the escutcheons of the Moslem Kings traversed with a band and motto. These glazed tiles, Azzulijas in Spanish, Azzulija in Arabic are of Oriental origin.

Their coolness, cleanliness and freedom from vermin render them admirably fitted in sultry climates for paving halls, and fountains. Encrusting bathing rooms and lining the walls of chambers. Ford is inclined to give them great antiquity. From their prevailing colors, sapphire and blue, he deduces that they may have formed the kind of pavements alluded to in the Sacred Scriptures. "There was under his feet as it were a paved work of sapphire stone," Exod. xxiv-10 and again. "Behold I will lay thy stones with the fairy colors and lay their foundations with sapphires."- Isa. IV-II. These glazed or porcelain tiles were introduced into Spain at an early date by the Moslems. Some are to be seen among the Moorish ruins have been there upwards of eight centuries. Manufactures of them still exist in the Peninsula and they are much used in the Spanish houses, especially in the southern provinces for paving and lining the summer apartments. The Spaniards introduced them into the Netherlands when they had possession of that country. The people of Holland adopted them with avidity as wonderfully suited to their passion for household cleanliness. And thus these Oriental inventions, the Azzulijas of the Spaniards, the Azzulija if the Arabs, have come to be commonly known as Dutch tiles.

By PROFESSOR DREW, The Egyptian Adept.

19. MOORISH LEADER'S HISTORICAL MESSAGE TO AMERICA

Friday, October 26, 1928

In connection with the aims, objects, rules and regulations of the Moorish Science Temple of America. I deem It proper to submit to you a brief statement of our organization, covering Its inception, rise and progress and of the Mohammedan religion, which I hope will be satisfactory to you and be the means of causing you at all times to adhere to the principles of Love, Truth, Peace, Freedom, and Justice in your relations with mankind in general. I further, most anxiously hope this brief statement will help you to more clearly see the duty and wisdom of at all times upholding those fundamental principles which are desired for our civilization of our posterity, such as obedience to law, respect and loyalty to government, tolerance, and unity.

We organized as the Moorish Temple of Science in the year of 1925, and were legally incorporated as a civic organization under the laws of the State of Illinois, November 29th, 1926. The name Moorish Temple of Science changed to the Moorish Science Temple of America, May 1928, in accordance with the legal requirements of the Secretary of the State of Illinois.

The object of our Organization is to help in the great program of uplifting fallen humanity and teach those things necessary to make our members better citizens.

A National organization with a Rotarian complexion as it relates to branch Temples became obvious with the increasing number of inquiries from men and women in different sections of the country concerning the purpose of the organization. There are branch Temples in fifteen (15) different states at this time.

Since the work of the Moorish Science Temple of America was largely religious, the organization has been legally changed to a religious corporation and an affidavit to this effect has been properly filed in the Cook County Recorder's office in Illinois.

Inspired by the lofty teachings of the Koran, we have it as the revealed word of God Allah. We shall foster the principles of its teachings among our members. This is our religious privilege as American citizens, under the laws of one of the greatest documents of all time-the American Constitution.

The Mohammedan religion is the least appreciated and probably the most misunderstood of the world's great religions. This is especially true in our western world. Try to understand what Mohammedanism stands for, and some of the things it has contributed to the world.

Mohammed was the founder of the Mohammedan religion. It originated thirteen centuries ago on the Arabian Peninsula, where the streams of commerce and culture met and mingled in the middle ages, where the markets of exchange were stationed for treasures of India and the products of the Mediterranean coasts. There, this religion was established in the unprecedented short period of twenty years, and unlike many other religions, without the aid of any royal patronage and support. Buddhism had its Asoka: Judaism its Joshua: Christianity its Constantine: but Mohammedanism had no person of royal rank and power to assist in its establishment and spread.

Today this religion is acknowledged by nearly two hundred and fifty million souls and extends over an area equal to one-third of the globe. From Arabia it spread eastward over Persia, Turkestan, Afghanistan, westward across Syria, Asia Minor, Turkey; southward to Africa, covering more than half of that continent. It found its way to India, and beyond, to the Islands of Sumatra, Java, and Borneo.

To the early representatives of this faith the world's debt is incalculably great. For it was they who transmitted the treasures of Greek literature from the middle ages to the Renaissance; they who originated the graceful forms of which the Taj mahal and the Alhambra are the most famous examples. It was they who contributed to the sciences of algebra and chemistry, astronomy, and medicine; they who dotted the Sarcen Empire with universities and who built at Bagdad and Cairo the most renowned universities of the world. During those centuries of ecclesiastical despotism when the Christian church suppressed all intellectual activities save those that were theological, causing the talent that reproduces to supplant the genius that creates. Mohammedans did all in their power to encourage and stimulate research in every branch of human inquiry.

The Moors or Mohammedans added to the beauty and grandeur of Spain. For centuries art, science, literature, and chivalry flourished among them, while the rest of Europe was still sunk in the gloom of the Dark Ages. The Moors were the most ingenious and industrious of the subjects of Spain. Their expulsion from Spain in 1610 was one of the chief causes of decadence of that country, for both agriculture and industry fell into decay after their departure.

Mohammedanism makes no distinction between high and low, rich and poor; it is like the sky, it has room for all.

The Koran should be of interest to all readers. It is the Bible of the Mohammedans, ruling over the customs and actions of over 200 millions of people. It is a work of importance whether considered from a religious philosophical or literary viewpoint.

In the promotion of plans for the betterment of mankind, there has ever been some kind of opposition. And strange as it may seem, such opposition has come from sources where there were no ideas or the lack of courage to force attention to ideas. Whether in church, state or the social community, any attempt to do anything out of the usual way, seldom fails to receive criticism. Not because the course cannot be pursued legally or that it is unreasonable, but because it has been considered in terms as new.

The Moorish Science Temple of America has received some opposition and criticism. In the main the opposition has come from certain Christian ministers. They have expressed themselves as being opposed to our propagation of the Mohammedan religion possibly because the promotion of the Mohammedan faith among our people in the United States is considered by them in terms as something new. Whatever the reasons may be for their opposition, the legal right to oppose citizens, individuals and organizations alike for their religious belief does not exist in the United States. The door of religious freedom made by the American Constitution swings open to all, and people may enter through it and worship as they desire. Without religious freedom, no search for truth would be possible; without religious freedom, no discovery of truth would be useful; without religious freedom, religious progress would be checked and we would
no longer march forward toward the nobler life which the future holds for the races of men; without religious freedom, there would be no inspiration to lift our heads and gaze with fearlessness into the vast beyond, seeking a hope eternal..

It is a sad weakness in us after all, to oppose our fellowmen for their religious beliefs, and if there are angels who record the sorrows of men as well as their sins, they certainly know how many and deep are the useless sorrows that spring forth from such opposition. Possibly, love and time will cancel our ancient hatreds in this regard and prove that in mankind, tolerance is better than unwarranted opposition.

In connection with our religious aims and beliefs, we must promote economic security. The preaching of economic security among us is by no means as widespread and intensive as the circumstances demand. No other one thing is more needed among us at this time than greater economic, power. Better positions for our men and women, more business employment for our boys and girls and bigger incomes will follow our economic security. We shall be secure in nothing until we have economic power. A beggar people cannot develop the highest in them, nor can they attain to a genuine enjoyment of the spiritualities of life.

Our men, women and children should be taught to believe in the capacity of our group to succeed in business, in spite of the trials and failures of some of them. Trials and failures in business are by no means confined to any particular group of people. Some business ventures of all people fail. We have many men and women among our people who are qualified, both by training and experience, who are shining lights in the business world of all the people. It is a sad weakness in us as a people that we have withheld the very encouragement, support and patronage that would have made some of our
worthy business ventures a grand success. And worst of all, have joined in the condemnations of them when they failed. Except in cases of actual dishonesty, discourtesy, lack of service and actual unreliability, our business enterprises in every field of endeavor should have lulled of confidence cooperation and patronage whenever and

wherever they can be given.

Read carefully the doctrines of The Moorish Science Temple of America. It contains our hopes, aims, rules and articles of religion. Every member should have a copy.

In conclusion, I urge you to remember there is work enough for all to do in helping to build a better world. The problems of life are largely social and economic. In a profound sense, they are moral and spiritual. Have lofty conceptions of your duties to your country and fellowman in general and especially those with whom you deal. This includes such honesty and righteousness as will cause you to put yourself in the other fellow's place. Look for the best in others and give them the best that is in you. Have a deeper appreciation for womanhood. Brighten the hopes of our youth in order that their courage be increased to dare and do wondrous things. Adhere at all times to the principles of love, truth, peace, freedom, and justice.

I am your affectionate leader. I shall continue to Labor Day and night, both in public and private, for your good, thereby contributing to the welfare of our country and its people as a whole.

NOBLE DREW ALI

20. SO THIS IS CHICAGO

Friday, October 26, 1928

All nations of the earth are now being forced to contribute their share in this American life. Some of the nation's here are put at a disadvantage supposedly because they happen to have a hue of every other nation of the globe. They have been victims of a peculiar psychology designed to hold them in mental slavery. So long as men permit other nations to furnish them with their food for thought just so long do they allow their heads to supplant their advisors.

What will happen among the Asiaitics of the world will first happen in The United States of America. And the first cosmopolitan city of this nation will be in Chicago. This is Chicago, the only city of the land that has all features of this American life engaged in by our people. Aldermen seated in the council of the city. Men high in official affairs of the city generally. There is but one Chicago.

21. POLITICAL SLAVERY

Friday, February 19, 1929

Anytime a Man or a Woman fails or refuses to cast a sacred ballot at the polls they separate themselves from all rights of an American citizen. For surely this is the one connecting medium for a citizen to his nation. They become no more than belated beast of burdens. There are reasons why certain classes, who are more or less independent, take no part in politics since they say they get nothing out of such in the way of material gain. This is no less than a political slave since they refuse to voice their sentiments at the polls. Another form of political slavery which is probably more prevalent among the less independent classes is that of being forced into one of the major parties and there bribed, coerced or otherwise forced to vote the wishes of someone else regardless of their own minds. Before there can be general relief for the economic good of all, all forms of political slavery must be abolished and every citizen must take his part in the affairs of the nation.

22. ALL REGISTERING

Friday, October 26, 1928

The three thousand Moslems of The Grand Temple and The West Side Temple are making ready to register every Man or Woman in order to take the lead for the various candidates whom they have been instructed to vote for. Alderman Louis B Anderson, Hon. George W. Blackwell, Hon. Oscar DePriest, Hon. H. Jackson, all working through the regular Republican Organizations of which The Hon. Daniel M. Jackson is our matchless leader all know the whole situation and have their own way and time to give the order to go. The Moslems will be ready.

23. TONGUES

Friday, February 1, 1929

One of the most difficult things in this world to get control of is the human tongue. Kipling never wrote anything truer than when he wrote that. "Man may hold most any post if he'll only hold his tongue". Before you set your tongue to action, get it under control. A single tongue can do more harm in the world than a battallion of soldiers. For soldiers can kill but bodies, while the tongue can kill reputations and characters. Really it is too bad that we have no laws to curb tongues from lying, and scandalizing. No doubt you all have read the story of Iago, a character in one of Shakespeare plays---when he powerfully pictured in the character of Iago the terrible consequences following the path of an evil tongue. Iago not only destroyed the reputation and pure character of Desdemona, but he finally, through Othello, killed her body. That's why I say--- compel your tongue to speak helpful messages or else--- keep it still. Make it a rule of your life to use your tongue for high purposes only. Resolve to speak of man or woman of no other way unless you speak of good qualities of that man or woman. No one ever gained happiness out of injuring the feelings or character of someone else. No one ever failed to get happiness by speaking well of other people. So learn as if you were to live forever-live as if you were to die tomorrow.

24. DREW ALI IN TIME

Friday, September 28, 1928

ALLAH has sent us a PROPHET and sent him in time with a Holy message which is divine. He came to let the Asiatics of America know they are of the ancient family of the MOORS. His spiel was to the Asiatics first. WHY? Because they have been sinners since their departure from their forefathers religion. OH! Sinners, why don't you hear the soul of Islam ringing in your ears. The Prophet has said that "if I were you I would get ready before you are made to do so". Now come and pick up your fore-fathers and mothers ancient and Divine creed which carries your national name indeed. It will entitle you to your rights which you have been denied. Because in 1774 your light was cut off from the ancient Moors and that is why ALLAH has sent to us a Prophet in 1886 to prepare the light that was out. In 1925 The Prophet said "I have mended the broken wires and have connected them with The Higher Powers." so come on Asiaitics, don't you want to go? We were marching on to Canaan. I used to think that it was a city in the sky, but now I know it is here on earth. DON'T YOU WANT YOUR SHARE?

25. MASTERPIECE OF RELIGIOUS LITERATURE: SECRETS OF OTHER CREEDS REVEALED

Friday, December 15, 1928

The Prophet, Noble Dew Ali has spent many hours preparing the latest edition of the Koran, which will be a masterpiece of Religious Literature. To Americanize the Oriental idea of Islam involves many changes that are more or less negative to the main purpose of the Islamic Religion. Such changes are carefully considered with the idea to avoid changing the complexion of the original text.

The philosophy of the ancient Prophets is the main initiative in the compilation of the Koran. No thoughts of propaganda enter this work, as has been the case of many former religious works, such as the Bible and other books of creed.

The sole purpose of the Prophet in giving such a message to the world is to save fallen humanity. When a compiler attempts to inject propaganda into a work of this kind, there arises a need to cover the true text in order to prevent a clash with the truth and ideas involved in such propaganda.

Former works of this kind have either hindered or helped the nations proportionately to the adherence to the truth as to the original purpose of keeping the ignorant in such a state. It is hard to resist the temptation to use this medium for gain. Hence, many of the former treaties on works of this kind have been the means to foster ideas of the unscrupulous wherein they desired to use religious influence for gain.

The many secrets known to the Prophet that could be used for the salvation of the nation were either left out or colored to an extent that their meaning was made void. Such is not the case with this edition of the Koran.

All the secrets of the ages known to man are put into this work. The secrets, known only to the Magi, are here revealed: the reading of the stars, the interpretation of marriage relations, the understanding of the span of life and other such as has been kept from the occidental world are in this book boldly brought out.

The Koran, Americanized as it will be, can be bought in a few weeks. It will be sent to all Governors of the Moorish Science Temples of America.

By Prophet Noble Drew Ali

26. TO BE PROCLAIMED AT EVERY MEETING

ISLAM:

I am glad to know that I have a few faithful Moors among you all, and I desire for them to know the Truth, and the Divine Truth. There is a host of Jealousy, about Me, and the Movement now by the same people of our side of the Nation that claim that I was only a joke and unreal; But now since they have found out from the Government Officials and the Nations of the Earth, that this is the only Soul Foundation, that all Asiatics must depend upon, for their Earthly Salvation as American Citizens, They are working every scheme that they can, to disqualify Me, so they may take charge of the situation.

I have notified all these things to you, long ago in the past. It is through the faithful Moors that attribute to the Movement and Uplifting Funds; the ones that paid their Divine respect to me and the Movement; will be remembered. That is why I am calling upon all faithful

Moors, to increase their faithfulness to Me Your Prophet, and You're Divine Moorish Movement.

I need finance, and I need it badly. Never before have I needed Finance so badly, as I do at present, so I can shove aside the Discord, that is facing the Nation. It all comes through Jealousy, Because of My Fame and Nobility. The Nations of the World will not recognize the movement, without I, The PROPHET, being Head. It has been proven by my works, which I have performed in the past few Years. - PROPHET NOBLE DREW ALI

27. TO THE MEMBERS OF THE MOORISH SCIENCE TEMPLE OF AMERICA

ISLAM:

This is the instruction from your Prophet Noble Drew Ali.

Be faithful unto your Forefathers Divine, and National Creed, that you will be blessed for your good deeds, that you sow in the flesh. "ALLAH" is the one that judges the World, and His judgment is now on. But the weak can comprehend it not. The end of Time is drawing near, so says "ALLAH" to His Divine "PROPHET I Noble Drew ALI". And that's why many hearts have been turned to stone, and many have Eyes to see, But cannot see, Ears to hear, But cannot hear. Least they would be confounded of their sins.

These are the trying hours now dear Moors, and every evil spirit is moving, And they are trying every weak mind, to overthrow and drag out the true foundation, that has been laid, and to cause confusion in the minds of the ones that do believe. But if you have the true Love of "ALLAH." And the spirit of your Forefathers, You fear not what you hear or see; but will sacrifice the utmost of your very life to protect your Movement and Your "PROPHET." Watch your

Enemies dear Moors; your enemies are the ones that speak against Your "PROPHET." And ridicule Him to the very lowest. And the ones that speak against "Your Divine and National Principles of Your Temples." Act accordingly, and "ALLAH" will bless you for your good work, "PEACE."

Your Divine PROPHET. "Noble Drew Ali."

28. OUR DOLLARS AND SENSE

The doctrine of economic security is by no means as widespread and intensive among Americans of our group as the circumstances demand, and the more written and said on the subject, the better.

We need to more earnestly urge conscientious support of the business men and women of our group in their chosen fields of endeavor. The greater the success of their business enterprises, the more open gates of opportunity there will be for our youth of today and tomorrow, Think of this fact we need to urge that our business men and women build on the principle of service. We! need to urge greater co-operation among them to render courteous, honest and efficient service to the buying public. They should not expect any support in patronage, merely on the grounds that they are race men and women in business, but for the reasons that the service and the quality of their goods and products they sell are equal in value to the service and merchandise offered to the buying public by any other business people. There should be maintained a co-operative spirit among our business men and women to keep their business places as clean and sanitary as any similar places in any other section of the city.

 Citizens of our group should cultivate a sound vision when it comes to the necessity of buying professional service, merchandise, provisions, etc.

We should look beyond the direct result and object for which we invest our money. We should lose sight of the mere fact that we received a dollar's worth for a dollar spent. We should keep firmly in mind the necessity of keeping each dollar spent as much as possible within the spheres of our own activities where they will create further openings of business enterprises and wider opportunities for the men and women of our group to procure soundly remunerative employment. Forward, must be the watchword of the seller and buyer alike. We make the money and we spend the cash. Let us sincerely cooperate one with the other. "Our plight will change when we change ourselves."

29. FOLLOWING OUR LEADERS

The thousands of Moorish Americans will follow their leaders. Regardless of propaganda put forth by those who have designs to hinder them in the work for the advancement of their people. We will not stop to question the requisites, qualifications nor anything else, so long as our leaders who have investigated and passed on the course of action which we feel is enough endorsement for us to act.

We have long known that the first attempt to crush the leaders of any movement or organization is to plant descention among their followers. Such will never will never be the case with the Moorish Americans, for when we have chosen our leader that within itself tells the world that we are going to follow them. All of the knocks and slams that come from anyone against our leaders will be ignored by us. Where they lead us we will follow.

30. DEDICATED TO THE SONS OF MAN

Amexem, the land of our Fathers; the land where the Gods love to dwell; the birthplace of the ancient Egypt-land;

where civilization first saw the light of day. Now since man has left his first religion he has been suffering from a complexed disease which in some way takes hold of his passions and desires.

The misdirection of his brain causes him to become a living monster; he is a slave to his lower-self. No scientist nor doctors have been able to find anything to affect a cure until the coming of Prophet Noble Drew Ali who comes from the east bringing the light of new day; the Moorish Divine Movement built upon love, truth, peace, freedom and justice; the salvation for the nation.

In the deliberation of nations no consideration is given to a people who are not of a nation. In 1774 the Europeans of this country took the birthrights away from a people whom they forced under bondage. They were not slaves; they were bound free men. The subsequent generation who followed them in this bondage were slaves because their minds had been subjugated to a European psychology. They were branded with the name Negro and were separated from the illustrious history of their forefathers who were the founders of the first civilization.

31. NICK NAMED

When the forefathers of the Moorish Americans were first brought to this nation they had a nationality and a name, but in order to separate them from the achievements of their fathers a name was given them which had no connection whatever with the founders of civilization. They were nick-named "negroes". Today in this nation there are no such things as Negroes in this sense that they are called: Just why so many of the intelligent Americans will continue to cling to this nick-name is hard to understand.

If you look in some dictionaries you will see that the word Negro means a sly person; a coon. If this is not an insult to the illustrious history of a nation there can never be one given. Just as thy have saddled on the Moorish Americans the name Negro they have also given him a religion that was made to enslave him and stop his progress. It is the duty of every man who lives to redeem the name of his forefathers and not be herded in to a mass of weaklings. Stop referring to yourself as Negro, colored and black for you are neither. If you are men, American citizens speak up for yourselves or it will never be done.

As long as you wear the clothes of another, or live in the house of another, or depend on another in any manner you are truly a slave to them. If you would be free indeed you must seek the truth. You must know the truth of your nationality and the name of your people; you must not be a coward and deny yourself the personal rights that belong to every man.

32. DEMANDING OURS

The idea inculcated in the purposes of the Moorish Science Temple of America is to have everything that belongs to us as a nation that has become part of another nation, just the same as all other European groups are doing.

We must have the history of our fore-fathers taught to our children. We have ceased to calculate our history from the landing of the "First Twenty" or the close of the Civil War. While all records of the tombs in the old world are proclaiming our glory to the nations, we have come now demanding that we be given credit for the great work done in the past by our ancestors. We are not asking others to give these records to the world for us but we demand that such records be broadcasted to the four winds by us and for us.

A pride that goes with the knowledge of great deeds will serve to cause our posterity to take heart and look into the vast future with a hope eternal. Such can never be done except they be taught who they are and where they are from. Yes, we are demanding that these things be done and we know that it will require some time before we have created that consciousness in others of our group to assert themselves likewise but that day is coming when such will be the case.

33. HISTORY DEFINED

History may be defined in a general way as the record of the life of mankind. It is the rise and progress of those famous people whose doings constitute the history of civilization.

In this, its proper and highest science, history presupposes the nations of the world advanced beyond the natural or primitive state and to these belong our Great Leader Mohammed directed by our Father God, Allah.

Respecting mankind outside of nations there is much interesting and valuable knowledge supplied by various sciences. By the aid of these sciences much is now known regarding mankind's customs, manners, languages, arts and religions which bring us back to our Father Allah and the moslem religion.

34. THE MOORISH SCIENCE TEMPLE OF AMERICA

The Moorish Science Temple of America was founded by the Prophet Noble Drew Ali. Aside from the fact that it is a legally organized religious corporation, It is building on human needs. To this desirable end, in time legitimate means will be found to dispense charity and provide for the mutual assistance of its members in times of distress; to aid in the improvement of health and to encourage the ownership of better homes; to find employment for our members; to teach those fundamental principles which are desired for our civilization such as obedience to law, respect and loyalty to government, tolerance and unity.

It is most earnestly hoped that the Moorish Science Temple of America, will not in any way be confused with any "Back to Africa Movement." Such is not important insofar as American citizens of our group colonizing Africa are concerned.

We, of the Moorish Science Temple of America, like countless other American citizens, know that we must live together here in America in harmony, friendship and goodwill, whatever our race and creed may be. It is only from a purely religious standpoint (it seems at this time) that we differ from a large number of our fellow Americans. We believe in, and foster the Moslem religion. We believe in the principles of its teachings insofar they can be adopted to American life. We feel that the Christian religion is alright for those who prefer it. In America, religious freedom is guaranteed all under the constitution.

We are Interested in freeing ourselves and our children, from the greatest plight- economic slavery. We believe this can be best done by encouraging, patronizing and establishing our own business enterprises and cultivating our own acres of land.

We welcome into our folds men and women of our group of all sections, all trades, occupations and professions of sound mind and good character.

We are friends and servants of humanity. We are dedicated to the purpose of elevating the moral, social, and economic status of our people. We have set about to do this through a wide and comprehensive program embodying the principles of love, truth, peace, freedom, and justice.

35. PROFESSOR DREW (in part)

Professor Drew

The Egyptian adept student.

181 Warren St. Newark, NJ.

I am a Moslem.

Professor Drew is a man who was born with Divine Power. He was taught the Adepts of Egypt. I have the secret of destroying the germs of tuberculosis and cancer of the lungs in 10 to 30 days.

Also give Divine Instructions and Interpretations of the Bible from genesis to revelations. Also have 18 years of Christ life that is silent to your Holy Bible for all those who desire to know more about Jesus the Christ.

36. MOORISH LEADER ATTENDS INAUGURATION OF GOVERNOR

The Moorish Science Temple of America was represented at the inauguration of Governor Louis L. Emmerson in Springfield, Ill, Monday Jan. 14 by Prophet Noble Drew Ali. It was a busy day for the distinguished Moorish leader in Springfield, beginning with breakfast aboard one of the special trains of the Illinois Central Railroad, attending the inaugural ceremonies of the State Arsenal building and ending with interviews with many distinguished citizens from Chicago, who greeted him on every hand. The Prophet expressed himself as being highly pleased with the trip and the many courtesies extended him by the military and state officials.

37. MOORS TO CELEBRATE BIRTHDAY OF FOUNDER

On the evening of Jan. 8 members of the Moorish Science Temple of America will celebrate Prophet Noble Drew Ali's birthday with a grand Moorish costume ball in the main auditorium of Unity Hall, 3140 Indiana Ave. The occasion will also be celebrated by all subordinate temples in other sections of the United States. The occasion will be the first of its kind in America, in that all members participating will wear native Moroccan costumes. A number of prominent men both in the business and public life of Chicago will join the members in honoring the Moorish leader's birthday.

38. MOORISH LEADER ON TOUR VISITS SUBORDINATE TEMPLES

Prophet Noble Drew Ali, Founder and Leader of the Moorish Science Temple of America, left Saturday to visit the members of 17 different subordinate Moorish Science Temples, which are organized in 15 different states. He is accompanied by Richard Ross Bey, editor of the Moorish Guide, a biweekly publication of the organization. Up-to-date Detroit, Newark, and Philadelphia have been visited. During this tour special emphasis is being put on the importance of strict observance by the members and officers of the constitution and by-laws recommended by the Prophet and unanimously adopted during the first annual convention of the Moors at Chicago in October 1928.

The message of the Prophet, published in the Moorish Guide issue of Nov. 10, has created very favorable comments. It was directed to the nations as well as the Moors of the United States. Two prominent visitors from an eastern country called at the Prophets private study, 3140 Indiana Ave. to personally compliment him on the article. According to information from Ms. Pearl D. Ali, national secretary treasurer of the Moors organization, members are responding encouragingly to the per capita tax system adopted at the convention. It is believed that in conjunction with his other plans, upon his return to Chicago, Prophet Ali, in all probability will interview Governor Len Small of the state of Illinois.

39. MOORISH HEAD MAKES PLANS FOR CONCLAVE

Beginning Oct. 15 and continuing through the entire week the Moorish Science Temple of America, of which MR. Drew Ali is the founder and president, will hold his first general conference at Unity Hall, 3140 Indiana Ave, Chicago Ill. President Ali began definite plans to this end upon his recent return from Pine Bluff, ARK, where he spent several days lecturing at the local Moorish temple.

This organization is playing a useful and definite part in advancing the sacred obligations of American Citizenship. Indications are that this convention will be one of the most interesting ever held in the city. It will be featured by delegates attending in pilgrimages from 15 different states where local temples have been established. There will be an interesting parade, in which men and women members will wear regalia similar to that worn in eastern countries. A camel will be used. During the sessions specific reports of the general work and civic accomplishments of local accomplishments will be made. Reports also of the business enterprises that have been established in connection with these temples, such as two grocery and market stores in Detroit, a laundry in Pittsburgh, PA, and moving and express business and grocery in Chicago.

These examples of collective effort show that the members of the Moorish Science Temple and their leaders have a sound economic program and are blazing the trail and marking the pathway over which our posterity may travel unhampered and unafraid. "It must be kept in mind that no great movement can take definite shape in two or three years so as to be error proof." said President Ali.

"However, through accumulating experience each annual convention ought to witness a more perfect a wider functioning organization, representing the organized experience of men and women members throughout the country and possibly in time the world over."

And continuing, President Ali said; "constructive criticism from sympathetic friends in and outside of our ranks is welcome."

40. HOLD SESSION OF MOORISH SCIENCE BODY

-Many delegates from temples attend-

The annual convention of the Moorish Science Temple of America opened Oct. 14 at Unity Hall, 3140 Indiana Ave. Prophet Noble Drew Ali, founder and head of the body will preside over the sessions, which closed Saturday evening. More than one thousand delegates from the 15 temples in America were reported present during the meetings.

Following the registrations at headquarters Monday reports were read from the two grand governors, T. Crumby Bey, Pittsburgh, Pa. and Lomax Bey of Detroit, Mi. Tuesday evening the welcome address was delivered by Alderman Louis B. Anderson. Other speakers were Oscar Depriest, third ward committeeman, Dr. Roman of Merharfy medical college Nashville, Tenn. Attorney George W. Blackwell and Aaron Payne. Richard Ross was master of ceremonies and Claude D. Green managing editor of the Moorish Guide, is chairman of the arrangement committee, which has worked hard to get everything in splendid order for the reception of the visitors. Wednesday a parade was held.

-Teaching Koran-

The Moorish Science Temple was founded by Prophet Drew Ali in Newark, NJ. in 1912. The tenets of the belief of his followers are that their forefathers were Asiatics brought to America along with all other persons of dark skin. They bar the name Negro, African or any allusion to color. They follow the teachings of the Koran, and movement toward free thinking is a powerful step toward the solution of racial problems. They teach strict cooperation and reciprocity towards each other;

The Chicago temple was organized in 1925 and has a membership of more than three thousand. The many hued turbans of the women and children and the red fez and sashes worn by the men attract much attention. Saturday a public recognition will be given in honor of the Prophet and the visitors.

Moorish delegates and visitors were served wholesome meals in the Unity Hall grillrooms by the members of the Chicago temple.

Sister Pearl Drew Ali, the distinguished wife of the Prophet wore the costume of a native Moroccan princess. Other very beautiful Moroccan costumes were worn by sister Lomax Bey, wife of the grand governor, of Detroit, sister Whitehead El, Chicago; sister Halsop Bey, Chicago; sister Cliff Bey, Indianapolis; sister Watts Bey, Chicago; and others. Prophet Noble Drew Ali wore a native Moroccan prince's costume. Grand Governor Lomax Bey and Grand Governor Crumby Bey wore native Moroccan sheik costumes.

Because of certain incidents in some of the branch temples previous to the convention, far reaching changes for betterment of the administrative affairs of the organization will be announced at the convention by the Prophet Noble Drew Ali and enforced by the supreme grand council in future to the laws.

-To make changes-

It is reported that the prophet, the supreme executive authority will appoint a supreme grand council of which he will be the Supreme Grand Chairman. The Supreme Grand Council will have power and duty to control and supervise all the affairs and properties of the Moorish Science Temple of America, and they will be the sole judge of what constitutes conduct injurious to the order, peace, interest or welfare of the organization, or at variance with its constitution and by-laws, also the rules and regulations made by the Prophet, and shall be the sole judge of the sufficiency of the evidence by which such conduct is shown.

Prophet Noble Drew Ali is being congratulated by Chicagoans on the success of the Moors first annual convention and for his splendid work to promoting the cause to humanity.

41. TO ALL GOVERNORS, GRAND SHEIKS, AND HEAD OFFICIALS OF TEMPLES [1]

By order of Prophet Noble Drew Ali, has said the following thing during this our very first convention. Prophet Noble Drew Ali said that the Moorish Science Temple of America, was organized to play a useful and defined part in the advancement of the sacred obligation of American Citizenship, as the Moorish Divine National Movement was founded for the uniting of the Asiatic States of North America on May 1st, 1916 as this will have been our very first convention and most interesting one ever held in this city. It was featured by delegates from 15 different states, from local Branch Temples and Subordinate Temples, which have been established for the Uplifting of Fallen Humanity.

During this our first convention, in sessions specific of general work and civil accomplishments were reported by the Grand Sheiks of each Branch Temple and Subordinate temple. As each Grand Sheik was required to give a reporting of his temple, and the Governor and in the continued growth and development of this Divine Movement. As each Grand Sheik gave their report about the growth of business and enterprises of the example of collective efforts, show that the members of the Moorish Science Temple of America and their leaders have enacted a sound economic program and are blazing the trail and marking the pathway over which our posterity can travel unhampered and unafraid.

Prophet Noble Drew Ali stated that it must also be kept in mind that no great movement can take definite shape in two or three years so as to be error proof. Prophet Noble Drew Ali further stated, "However, through accumulating experience each annual convention ought to bear witness a more perfect and wider functioning organization, representing the organized experience of men and women members throughout the country and possibly in time the world over and continuing Prophet Noble Drew Ali said, "constructive criticism from sympathetic friends in and outside of our ranks is welcome."

42. TO ALL GOVERNORS, GRAND SHEIKS, and HEAD OFFICIALS OF TEMPLE. [2]

During this convention period the Prophet Noble Drew Ali said, on the 17th of October, that he was going to appoint seven men tried and true and accepted by you and on the very next day Noble Drew Ali step forward from the chamber room and declared that he now had his number, and said that the Grand Body had accepted his choice in the setting of the Supreme Grand Council of the Moorish Science Temple of America and Prophet Noble Drew Ali also declared what their duties in conjunction with that of the Grand Body which consist of all Executive Rulers [Chief Rulers, Governor].

Prophet Noble Drew Ali said that both are to work hand in hand with each other, and those who act as in a Supreme Council duties were to continue on with each other, and those who act as in a Supreme Council duties were to continue on with the day to day functions of this Divine Movement. While the Grand Body was to intercede that the Prophet Noble Drew Ali was the law, and at the head of this Divine Movement.

Now the Prophet Noble Drew Ali announces that the following adept chamber members would be seated on the Supreme Grand Council.

1. Prophet Noble Drew Ali, Supreme Head and Supreme Chairman

2. Bro. Edward Mealy El, Supreme Grand Sheik and Grand Governor, Temple #1

3. Bro. James Lomax Bey, Supreme Grand Governor and Grand Governor, Temple #4

4. Bro. Richard Ross Bey, Temple #1

5. Bro. C. Green Bey, Supreme Business Manager, Temple #1

6. Bro. Blackwell Bey, Temple #1

7. Sis. Pearl Ali, Supreme Grand Secretary, Temple #1

Then Prophet Noble Drew Ali said "follow me and you will be happy". The Prophet also announced that a per capita tax had been voted in by the Grand Body and concurred with by the Supreme Grand Council, during the second sitting of the Supreme Grand Council."

43. TO THE HEADS OF ALL TEMPLES

Islam,

These are critical moments, and all Moslems are required to follow instructions.

During the life of our Prophet, he told us many things, but there was many things that he said he couldn't tell, but we would know after a while.

Since he passed he left his son who will guide you, now of course the Prophet's laws are alright but there are plenty he couldn't write or put in book form, so someone had to tell you, now some are going to believe it and some are not, but now let me say to you as a brother we loves Israel, please don't be the hardhead.

In the Adept last night we were told not to eat meat, but to eat anything in the fish line with scales on it, that leaves out cat and eel, eat fish and vegetables, etc. but no meat of any kind or any strong drinks until further notice.

Please don't do any of these things until you hear from the Grand Body.

PEACE,

Your Brother in Islam

E. MEALY EL. S.G.S.

44. TEMPLE NO. 11, 817 SOUTH BROAD STREET

Friday, August 14, 1929

Bro. A. H. Payne-El, S.B.M.
3757 South State Street,
Chicago, Illinois

Dear Brother Payne-El,

In reading your letter to Brother Thompson-El a few minutes ago, and in view of the wishes of our PROPHET, as laid down in his laws to me, by himself, I wish to call tour attention to the fact that it was his will that we hold the coming convention of 1929, beginning September the 15th to the 20th of the same month.

My objection is only that the date which was made by the PROPHET be considered as law with me. And remembering also that he said; "as long as you do what I tell you, you will be alright. But when you fail to obey my orders, you will have trouble." having talked the matter over with all the Governors, I find them all in favor of supporting the date of the Convention as laid down by our PROPHET.

Now, as Business Manager, I am asking you to give away to the time of the PROPHETS choice and arrange your dates accordingly, which begins September 15th to September 20th inclusive. This will also give them more time for preparation for the same.

We must do all we can for Peace, that a progressive advance may manifest itself in all of our actions. This done, all also is well. Trusting this meets your approval, I am
You're Brother in Islam,

E. MEALY EL S.G.S.

45. MARCH 11, 1929

Brother Crumbey-Bey the Governor and Chief Head of the Temple in Pittsburgh Pa. Brother Childs-Bey Governor and Chief Head of the Temple in Cleveland Ohio.

These two Brothers are in power by the PROPHET to investigate business etc. of Temple number four in Detroit Michigan, because Lomax-Bey has violated all DIVINE LAWS of the PROPHET even before the Prophets face Feb. 15 1929. He claims that the Prophet has no more power and the finance from Detroit would be in his charge. He wouldn't send any to the Prophet.

He yelled with a loud voice, "Look at me. I will guide you through." This is lawful and living evidence spoken before fifteen hundred (1500) people and the Prophet was also present.

I, THE PROPHET, declare his office vacant and the name of Grand Governor discharged. He can only be a member according to LAW because the Moorish Science Temple of America is a DIVINE ORGANIZATION. Each Temple is under Supreme Guidance of the Prophet.

When man fails after being placed Head of the Temple by the Prophet of obeying our Divine laws and constitutions, he is a traitor and enemy of the Divine Creed and Unloyal to the National Government U.S.A. to which the movement is to make men and women better citizens.

FROM THE PROPHET,

NOBLE DREW ALI.

46. FORESTERS HALL, 44th AND STATE STREET

Friday, September 26, 1930

ISLAM,

Bro. C. Kirkman Bey, this is to notify you, that the above named Organization, MOORISH SCIENCE TEMPLE OF AMERICA, in Convention, SEPT. 15th to 20th, resended by voting out the mistake made by the second annual Convention, of 1929.

And in so doing, you hold your Membership Roll, as when our Prophet was here, and we hope you will still cooperate with the organization under the five principles.

We hope further, that you will comply with this notice, and govern yourself accordingly.

As there is but ONE Supreme Grand Adviser, in the MOORISH SCIENCE TEMPLE OF AMERICA, that being NOBLE DREW ALI, and anyone else attempting to be, from now on, is assuming authority of himself, and is liable to the penalties of the LAW.

PEACE.

MOORISH SCIENCE TEMPLE OF AMERICA

NOBLE DREW ALI, FOUNDER.

E. MEALY EL, CHAIRMAN

47. THE GREAT MOORISH DRAMA

DONT MISS THE GREAT MOORISH DRAMA

LOOK! LOOK!

COME YE EVERYONE AND SEE

THE SEVENTH WONDER OF THE WORLD

The Great Moorish Drama, which constitutes

"EVENTS IN THE LAST DAYS AMONG THE INHABITANTS OF NORTH AMERICA"

In this Moorish Drama the need of a nationality will be made known to you through the acts, of men, women and children. There will be great lectures and this nationalistic topic by the Prophet Noble Drew Ali, and many of the Sheiks of the Grand Body of the Moorish Holy Temple of Science. You will also hear one of the greatest Moorish female songstresses of the day -- MME LOMAX-BEY.

THE PROPHET NOBLE DREW ALI, WILL BE BOUND WITH SEVERAL YARDS OF ROPE, AS JESUS WAS BOUND IN THE TEMPLE AT JERUSALEM

And escaped before the authorities could take charge of Him; so will Prophet Drew Ali, perform the same act, after being bound by anyone in the audience and will escape in a few seconds.

H also will heal many in the audience without touching them, free of charge, as they stand in front of their seats manifesting his divine power.

COME ONE, COME ALL TO

THE MOORISH HOLY TEMPLE OF SCIENCE

AT COMMUNITY CENTRE

3140 INDIANA AVE.

8 to 11 p.m. Refreshments served.

ADMISSION: ADULTS 50c CHILDREN 25c

ON MONDAY EVENING, MAY 16TH, 1927

Made in the USA
Middletown, DE
18 October 2023

41065642R00035